About the Authors

The Latino Outreach Leaders (LOL) are a student organization that began at Dunbar High School by a group of youth who recognized the need for student leadership among the Latino community in Lexington, Kentucky. Their mission is to help Latino students through outreach, education, and recreation.

The Latino Outreach Leaders

Students: Ana Castillo, Ana Contreras, Nydia Cordero, Maria Eugenia Cordero Barrios, Armando Diaz, Willie Diaz, Yasuri Diaz, David Dominguez, Edson Gonzáles, Merari Gonzáles, Noemi Lara, Gisselle Lopez, Erika Nuñez, Maria Ortiz, Jose Paredes, Luis Paredes, Ricardo Perez, Francisco Rodriguez, Bryan Salas, Antonio Sanchez, Kevin Sibaja, and Jesus Valencia

Faculty Sponsors: Jim Adams, Sharessa Bentley-Crovo, Tabatha Doyle, Sarah Maxwell, and Cathy Yaun

Living Out Loud:
Our Stories, Our Struggles
Edited by Steven Alvarez

Wordography

Published by Wordography, with support provided by the University of Kentucky and the publication unit of the Division of Writing, Rhetoric, and Digital Studies and the Department of English.

Address all editorial inquiries to: Writing, Rhetoric, and Digital Studies, University of Kentucky, c/o English Department, Lexington, KY 40506-0027

Library of Congress Cataloging-in-Publication Data

Latino Outreach Leaders

Living Out Loud: Our Stories, Our Struggles by the Latino Outreach Leaders—1st ed. p. cm.

ISBN-13: 978-1-48275-384-4

ISBN-10: 1-48275-384-7

Cover illustration: *Hunger* by Maria Ortiz

Typeface: Verdana

Produced and printed in the United States of America

If you want to know what we are, look upon the farms or upon the hard pavement of the city. You usually see us working or waiting for work, and you think you know us, but our outward guise is more deceptive than our history.

Our history has many strands of fear and hope, that snarl and converge at several points in time and space. We clear the forest and the mountains of the land. We cross the river and the wind. We harness wild beast and living steel. We celebrate labor, wisdom, peace of the soul.

—Carlos Bulosan, *Freedom from Want*

Contents

Images

Dedication

This book is dedicated to all the families and individuals
struggling to achieve the Dream,
and to our families struggling to achieve our Dreams.

Acknowledgements

The Latino Outreach Leaders would first like to thank all the faculty and students of Paul Laurence Dunbar High School for their continued support. They also thank Latino Outreach and Services Coordinator Erin Howard of the Office of Multiculturalism and Inclusion at Bluegrass Community and Technical College and the Kentucky Latino Education Alliance for their continued guidance. The differences Erin and K'LEA have made in the lives of countless Latino youth in Kentucky are immeasurable. In addition, LOL thanks the Kentucky Dream Coalition for sharing the power of stories. The Village Branch Library and Lexington Hispanic Association also deserve thanks for their community programs, as many LOL students benefitted from these. LOL also thanks Harold Gonzalez, Lexmark, and the Kentucky Bluegrass Professional Chapter of the Society for Hispanic Engineers and the Lexington Hispanic Association for their mentorship and sponsorship of various events. LOL also wants to publically acknowledge Dunbar High teachers Jim Adams, Sharessa Bentley-Crovo, Tabatha Doyle, Kim Overstreet, and Beverly Henderson as exemplary educators. Finally, LOL thanks the Department of English and the Division of Writing, Rhetoric, and Digital Studies at the University of Kentucky for sponsoring this project.

Living Out Loud:
Our Stories, Our Struggles

Introduction

Waves

Sharessa Bentley-Crovo

During class I gave my usual speech about how it doesn't matter where you come from, how much money you have, or what neighborhood you live in, education can take you anywhere you want to go in life. Once you have it you will be empowered to do great things. The students were asking about college and how can you pay if they didn't have any money. I told them if they had the grades to get in, there were scholarships, grants, and student loans. One of my Latino students quickly interrupted me and reminded me that he didn't have the same opportunities as everyone else because he was not a U.S. citizen.

I had never had a student bring this up.

I felt terrible that I was rallying everyone in the class and telling them they had all these opportunities for higher education, but now realized I was leaving an increasing amount of students I taught. I realized this student felt he was not good enough for college, that he felt like he did not deserve an education. He explained to me that it was easier for a young person without "papers" to find money and protection by joining a gang or selling drugs. I hear him now: "Why work hard getting an education when you cannot do anything with it? You have to have a social to get FAFSA money and you have to have a social for anyone to hire you."

And he wasn't alone. I met several students in the same predicament. I realized I had to do something different or lose several of my students for the rest of the year. There was no way they were going to try in my class or any class if they knew they would not be able to apply their educations later in their lives. Many questions rapidly ran through my mind. Why didn't anyone tell the teachers what was going on? What kind of preparation had been done to help this growing population?

The next day I pulled several students into the hall and asked them, "What if I can find a way for you to go to college, would you try more in class?"

They said, "yeah, but you won't."

I told them I looked forward to the challenge.

It was a deal.

There had to be a loophole for these road-blocked students to get a college education. They were just as smart as anyone else, and they wanted to learn. They were brought to the United States because of decisions their parents made for better opportunities, not because they wanted to break the law, but to make better lives. Some of the students did not even remember living in their home country. I thought that if I could find a way, I might prevent some of these students from at least joining a gang, and maybe even get them a chance to go to college.

Finally, I stumbled on a website entitled "The Kentucky Dream Coalition." I read their blog posts and saw all of the things they were doing to help young undocumented people. I felt like I had finally found a way to help my students. Not only was there legislation that was being proposed to help young people in this very situation, but there were also colleges around the country that offered free classes, assisted students with becoming legal citizens, and helped them find jobs in their fields of study. I also found contact information for people in charge of Latino Outreach at local colleges and universities. By Monday I was armed with an abundance of resources to share with the students.

They could not believe that I had found out such information in two short days. We read the research together and we agreed that Dreamer students had to get good grades and keep a clean record. They started staying after school to improve their grades. This group eventually turned into the Latino Outreach Leaders.

I followed through with my end of the deal so they had to follow through with theirs, and they exceed my expectations. The local college's Latino Outreach began emailing me about a program they were putting together called Dream University. They wanted to offer free classes for Latino students, and they needed teachers to volunteer to teach them.

I signed up because it further encouraged students to get an education and showed them good citizenship by volunteering. I asked if my high school students could attend, and they agreed it would be a great experience for them. That following day I told them about Dream U and invited them to come to the class. Most of them were so excited something like this was being offered. Many had excuses of "I can't," and "I don't have a ride." I gave them bus fare and asked, "How bad do you want this?" I always tell them, "If you want something bad enough you make it happen, if it's not a priority than there are excuses."

Ironically the class I decided to teach at Dream U was about social movements. There was no sleeping. Students were participating and comparing movements like the Civil Rights Movement to their own lives. We talked about how past generations had faced discrimination and how people have used positive actions to change the culture of the society we live in. There were classes covering many subjects (art, language, communication, government, and history). It was like a light had been turned on. The LOL students also found other opportunities while networking at the college campus among other students in the same situation. There were many students from our high school who had already been working with the Dream Coalition. The Kentucky Dream Coalition invited students to get involved with the Spanish Honor Society as well. High school students started taking part in artwork activities, the local Hispanic Heritage Festival, and participated in our local parade with the Dream Coalition. Instead of feeling like invisible citizens, they were becoming active members.

In the years that have followed our LOL program has blossomed into an advocacy group for all students who are in need of resources to be successful. The students and I have witnessed a new coming of age immigration policy with Deferred Action and changing attitudes toward aspiring immigrant youth. Many people do not realize these youth are in all communities, and unfortunately for many their obstacles are invisible. But their problems are every community's problems, and their obstacles are community obstacles. We have to learn to embrace these youth as the next generation of teachers, doctors, lawyers, and professionals . . . as leaders.

In order to teach such youth to be productive members of society, society must first make them feel that they are members. In order to achieve this, our school and community have created outlets for our immigrant students to succeed. With the help of local advocacy groups, libraries, and colleges, these youth have found acceptance and guidance. Over the last four years the LOL students have developed into productive, self-confident students. The sky is the limit, and they are making waves.

Learning the Language of Teaching

Tabatha Doyle

I grew up in a small town where the most diverse person was the woman who had did the "unforgivable" and had a baby with her Black boyfriend. I lived a sheltered life where the only color was White. In this small town in Eastern Kentucky, no one was bilingual. I went through twelve years of school without a foreign language and feeling scared of the diversity that existed outside of the small bubble we had created.

When I went away to college, I was in shock at how many different people there were, and I was somewhat scared of the fact that I was no longer in the safety of my hometown. For me at this time, foreign was scary.

It didn't help that I had to take Spanish class. I had made it through 18 years of my life only speaking English. Bilingualism wasn't something anyone considered where I grew up. The folks in my town were more the "Why don't they just learn English?" variety. But nonetheless I struggled through my first year of college-level Spanish classes in order to fulfill my university studies foreign language requirement. I struggled, and improved, but I realized I wanted to learn more Spanish as it began to interest me. During my second semester, I learned about an opportunity to learn Spanish in Mexico. On a whim, I went for it. I wanted to see more of the world and to practice what I learned.

Upon arriving in Mexico, I was numb to everything around me, and for a few days I struggled with the differences. As time went on, I began to adjust and realized that what I once saw as differences were really likenesses. In Mexico, I met caring people in a community that resembled mine in Kentucky. I came to know people who were striving to take care of their families, willing to help no matter what. I realized that I loved the Mexican culture and the importance Mexicans gave to family. My eyes were opened to the rewards of learning Spanish, and how just by learning a new language, I was also learning a new culture that I have been accepted into with open arms

After many days, years, and tears in Mexico, I am now a Spanish teacher and I get to share my love of the Spanish language and culture and hopefully plant the seed of acceptance that was planted in me during my time in Mexico.

I have always said that I have the best job in the world. I get to wake up every morning and do something not because I have to, but because I want to. During my time at Dunbar, I have not only fulfilled my life calling, but I have also taught some of the most amazing students I have ever met. The highlight of my week comes each Wednesday when I meet with the Latino Outreach Leaders. They are a fantastic group of students who have demonstrated to be community leaders. They will all do beautiful and important things. I know that each one of these students will effect positive changes in the world. In twenty years when I look back on these times, I will see that Kentucky is better because of the differences that they made.

Dragon by Bryan Salas

Learning To Be Myself
Jose Paredes

I was never the one to fit in properly. I always wanted to get along with everyone, but as I grew up I noticed racial tensions between different groups of people. I started to notice all of the negative stereotypes and how they impacted my image of myself. In elementary school, I was just learning English and I was making new friends, but as I went on to middle school, I discovered that my classmates didn't think much of Mexicans. I was viewed as an innocent child in elementary school, but when I got to middle school I became a "wetback."

This didn't affect me bad as I thought. I just acted myself, and the negative stereotypes disappeared for me. As I went into high school, everything changed—including me. The negative stereotypes resurfaced. I was eager to continue my studies in high school, but it wasn't easy with all of the people expecting and waiting for me to mess up and fail— to fulfill the stereotype. Just because I was a Latino, people expected that I was uneducated, that I didn't speak English, and that I had just crossed the Mexico-U.S. border. That's not the kind of image I had of myself, but the image I was given. I was perceived as a "wetback" once again.

I did my best to avoid the negative stereotypes. At first I tried so much to fit in: I bought nice clothes, tried to act different, and in one case tried drugs. This wasn't me, though. Over the years, I noticed I made a worse image for myself. I still had outstanding grades, but they were decreasing from my lack of motivation. That's when I went down a different path. I stopped worrying about what others thought about me, found my own style, and started to better myself in my studies and behavior. I also worked to make a positive image for Latinos, as driven, smart, and academically successful. Soon after, no one saw me as a "wetback"—they saw a classmate and friend.

I don't regret what I did to fit in because it taught me a very valuable lesson. I learned that I don't have to have the nicest clothes, a cool car, or be "bad" to fit in. I just needed to be myself. And those who would become my friends, then, would be the ones who really cared about me.

My Motivations

Maria Ortiz

I am a person who has come from humble origins as I put in the effort to climb up the ladder and achieve success in everything I do. I have had many bright moments at school; however, I shine brightest when it comes to creating visual pieces that send some sort of message. Nonetheless, my talent, my roots, my experiences, and my beliefs all motivate me to finish my work in a thorough manner.

I spend large amounts of my time creating things that the world has never seen, through materials that the world is used to seeing. I feel the need to create which makes me believe that I was put on this earth to make it beautiful. Everyone is drawn to what is aesthetically pleasing. Art is also made to make people think in order to change their minds, thus collectively changing the way society works. But it also has its purpose to entertain and, most importantly, to renew people's lives. Overall, art is such a powerful force because it is a form of knowledge. Though it is unappreciated in society, I still have the ardor and the stubbornness to continue what I love to do. Nevertheless, I would not have the passion that I do if it wasn't for the environment I grew up in.

I was born in Zacatecas, Mexico and because of the poverty that my parents had to deal with, they decided to move to the United States when I was three. As I grew older, I realized all that my parents gave up in order for me to have a better life. However, I recognize that I am in a country of abundance and wealth, so I try to stay humble and remember where I came from. My parents greatly encourage me to strive for success. I always force myself to be self-disciplined and self-motivated. I also always try to be well-rounded. I dislike focusing on just one form of education because I feel like I am missing out on other activities that I would most likely enjoy. This goes the same for the art that I make. I try to branch out and be as well-rounded as possible. My love for art began at a young age when I discovered the satisfaction I got from painting. This grew into an obsession with learning how to draw things well. Since then, I have given printmaking and ceramics a try. I am not as successful in those two forms of art, but at least I now know that it's not my thing. My work is mostly conceptual because I believe that art is meant to have meaning. I try to find an abstract importance in everything due to my belief that critical thinking makes art more valuable. However, there are times when art should just be art without a certain connection tied to it. Some pieces should exist just for aesthetic purposes.

When a person is given a gift as special as the gift of creativity, then I believe that it must be shared with the rest of the world. When I was younger, people would tell me to draw things for them. This always made me feel very special, and I was never reluctant to turn an ordinary piece of paper into something beautiful, especially if it pleased someone else. As I grew older, I began doing work for larger purposes. I have done several murals for my community. I began working on a larger scale my sophomore year in high school where every student in my two-dimensional art class had to create a design for a certain section of the school. Only five designs would be made into real murals. I never thought that my piece would be one of those five, but as fate would have it, my design grew into a wall-sized piece. Later that year, a local artist was hired to paint a mural on the side of the public library. I was on the design team to do this. We collaborated on the mural. I made a suggestion that the design should be changed by a small amount so the piece would flow together better. The design team went along with my suggestion. I cannot describe the wonderful and fulfilling emotions I experience when I walk by these murals and realize that a piece of me will permanently reside there.

I began taking art seriously when I applied to Governor's School for the Arts. It is a very competitive three-week summer program where over 2,000 students apply. Yet only 250 are accepted. I was one of these very fortunate students who got in. It was at this program when I realized that creating was something that I must do for the rest of my life. This was how I wanted to live and who I wanted to be: an artist.

Sometimes I have an easier time explaining myself in pictures rather than words because words can be so messy and complicated. Pictures speak for themselves as there is almost never a time where meaning gets lost in translation. My ideas are derived from personal experiences that most often correlate to music. I am also very in tune with several social issues that greatly matter to me. I try to spread knowledge and dissipate ignorance about these social issues through visual means.

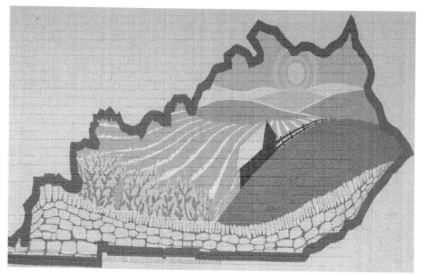

Cardinal Valley mural by Luella Pavey and local Lexington, Kentucky youth, including Maria Ortiz

Join the Dance

Erika Nuñez

Let your spirit fly
Take in this sweet melody
Just move with the beat—
Won't you care to dance?

Raise your arms high—
Can you feel the soft sky?
Step, step souls dance—
Laughter and smiles fill the room

Bodies move entranced by music—
Freedom reigns through the night.
There's no need to hurry—
Won't you join the dance?

Take my hand!
Don't be afraid—
Let your spirit in—
Everything's going to be okay.

Now see what you feel—
Look up!
There, can you see the feelings?
Don't fear—I'm right here—
Won't you care to dance?

Shifting songs—
No lyrics.
Nothing but the beat—

Hurry doesn't exist.

Dance like no one else. *cheesy, but*
This is your time. *true*
Your dream.
Won't you join the dance?

Mexicans

David Dominguez

My mom is patient and calm. My dad passed away. I got four sisters, three are older and one is younger than me.

My dream is to become famous and teach kids how to perform as actors and actresses. I already started making videos so people can recognize me, I just made my first video yesterday.

Violence is something that Latinos are mostly using to stop themselves from achieving their goals. Being afraid to reach that goal, many Latinos don't go to college because they always think to themselves "I'm a Latino, and Latinos don't go to college . . . why should I?" Many people notice that, and they are racist because when they see a Latino trying to make a business, people like that believe that the chances of Latinos having a good business are not possible.

I am a Mexican, and I see myself as an example to the people that are trying to look down at us. When I learned English, it was hard. People looked down on me when I tried to speak English because I had an accent, and I talked Spanglish hoping for them to understand what I said. But eventually I learned to express myself and stand up for myself.

And Sometimes Not Say Anything

Ana Contreras

I came to the United States when I was five. I didn't want to come here at first because I didn't know anything about this country. It was my parents' choice though I didn't have any say in this. We got here, and when I started school it was a struggle for me because I didn't understand any English. I would talk in Spanish to the teacher or sometimes not even say anything.

Growing up we moved around to several houses until we got settled at a farm. I hated it more there. I was about eight when we moved to the farm. I thought *how I could go from Mexico to Lexington, Kentucky and living on a farm?* My life was already bad enough to be here.

I missed Mexico especially my aunt who was also like my second mother growing up. My mother couldn't really take care of my brothers and me especially since I had a twin brother. I went and lived with my aunt until I started calling her mom and my father got mad then took me back. When I was old enough, my parents brought me over to the United States. I missed my aunt so much and talking to her on the phone wasn't the same as being with her. A few years later she passed away—the person that meant everything to me. I was about thirteen or fourteen when she died. I hadn't seen her for eight years, and I will never see her ever again. This still makes me sad. I blamed my parents for bringing me here. I could have been with my aunt taking care of her, and maybe she wouldn't be gone.

I rebelled against my parents. I didn't listen. I skipped school. I never did any drugs or smoked. I just didn't want to go to school. I wasn't happy. I was young then, and now I'm 17, about to turn 18. Now I can appreciate everything my parents have done bringing me over here for better opportunities. I regret skipping school and being bad, and how that affected my future. Now I am trying so hard to bring my

GPA up and do better in school. I love school. I just didn't back then.

I struggled a lot in this country. I had a hard time because I missed my aunt so much that I couldn't see how wonderful this place was. Now this is my home. I know nothing of Mexico besides that I was born over there, but this is where I'm from. I'm Kentucky. I've been here for nearly my whole life.

Palmetto Park by Maria Ortiz

Mi Mamá

Jose Paredes

My mom is the best, she's amazing. She's the most hard-working woman I know. I don't know where I would be without her. She works her butt off to feed her kids. She's always so tired and out of energy. She just recently lost her job so it's been kind of hard lately. But I'm glad I'm working now, and I can help her. It gives me the greatest joy to see her smile—she is the best. I'm happy to be able to help her.

My big dream is to be able to supply my mom with everything she needs. To be able to buy her a house, have maids—so she wouldn't have to lift a finger. My dream is basically to succeed, to make someone out of myself, to go farther than anyone can go.

I feel like community is one big factor why Latinos fail, because many don't do anything with their lives due to their peers holding them back. If your best friend doesn't go to college it will make you consider not going either. If your friends do drugs, that shows you that drugs aren't bad, so you start to do drugs. If we choose our friends better, we would choose the path for ourselves.

The number one factor that will hinder my success: citizenship. I wasn't able to do anything. I couldn't drive anywhere because I didn't have a license. I couldn't apply to jobs because I didn't have a valid social. But now all that has changed thanks to Deferred Action, DACA. I am a Latino. I'm proud. But I feel like I am not the best example of what my people could be. I don't express this much because I don't want to be looked down upon and because I want to stay positive.

When people see Mexicans, they see a non-English speaking "wetback," and I don't want anyone to look at me like that. I want people to know me by my name not my color. I hang out with everyone, and I'm too Mexican for white people, but I'm too *agringado* for Mexicans. It can be hard sometimes because so many Latinos think I'm ashamed of being Mexican but that's not the case.

Family

Willie Diaz

I got a big family. Most of them are from San Luis Potosí. *Somos Potosínos.* We love soccer, we love to eat, and chilling together. *Soy Potosíno.* I see myself as a hard-working Mexican.

Learning English was easy because I came here when I was turning three, and I learned English in daycare. Now I speak it more than Spanish, but I'm bilingual.

The biggest challenge for undocumented Latinos is not having green cards. Without a Visa and/or green card we can't apply for college and/or find a job because we don't have a social security number. We also can't apply for any government help because of illegal crossing and no legal documents. This gets in the way of success for some of us. And for those who have green cards, they don't care about those still struggling.

A Day I Will Never Forget

Noemi Lara

I started to look for my mom as soon as I heard the explosion. I could feel fear creeping up every part of me. I caught a glimpse of my mom, a tear came streaming down my face. It seemed as if in the blink of an eye, everyone ran towards her. I stood there in shock, feeling like a complete idiot for not being able to help her out. *Do something!* As my mouth filled with a bittersweet taste, I ran toward my mom. By the time I got to her my face was soaked in tears.

"Mamá, mamá!"

"Help her, somebody help her!" someone screamed.

"Someone get some water!"

"Help! Help!"

"Mamá, mamá!"

I cried out to her, and she told me not to be scared. But how could I? Only fear, that's all I felt, for the one who I loved most in this world.

Flashback to a few months earlier, July 2008. The Bluegrass Fair was coming up and my mom was investigating what she needed to become a food vendor. She knew this could be a big way to expand the Mexican restaurant she had built by herself. All I knew was that she was going to need a couple thousand dollars to pull off the whole thing. Since she had met all of the legal and health requirements she needed, it was time for my family to get prepared for some hard work up ahead. We were first-timers to all this commotion selling food at the Bluegrass Fair. After spending a whole afternoon and night setting up our booth, we were ready to start selling authentic Mexican food.

One of my mom's friends offered us his gas broiler so we could roast *al pastor* visible to the public. My mom didn't think twice in accepting the offer, but none of us knew what we needed to be very careful setting up this sort of appliance. Since it was a last minute addition, we hooked it up as best as we knew. On the fourth day of the fair, we were still having a lot of trouble with troubleshooting all the business we generated. Our food was a hit, but we were completely new and still learning the ropes. Other vendors had the advantage of years of experience. My mom was turning the *al pastor* when suddenly a loud explosion caught my mom on fire. Before I could even analyze what had just happened someone else had already come to the rescue and put her out.

Sometimes I would just lie on my bed and cry and reproach myself for not running to help her when it happened. I would pray to God and ask *Why mom?* Mom? It killed me inside to even think about the pain she was going through. I wish it would have been me instead of her. All along I had never realized how important my mother was to me until this happened.

Why do tragic things have to happen for people to understand the importance of others? After the accident, my aunt took care of my mom. My brother, sister and I went to work at the restaurant. We couldn't afford to have it closed down, especially with all the expenses we had to cover for my mother's care. While we worked I knew it crossed everyone's minds how my mother took on so much every day at work. It took three of us to do all the work she did on her own. I was amazed. I admired my mom's strength. She had the courage to get up every day and go to work for our well-being even if it meant she had to be in pain. That's something worthy to look up to.

A short while after this tragic experience, I knew that I didn't want to disappoint my mother, and I wanted to become someone with a bright future. It is for her that I want to accomplish great things in life and further my education. I want to be someone that inspires many people, just like she inspired me.

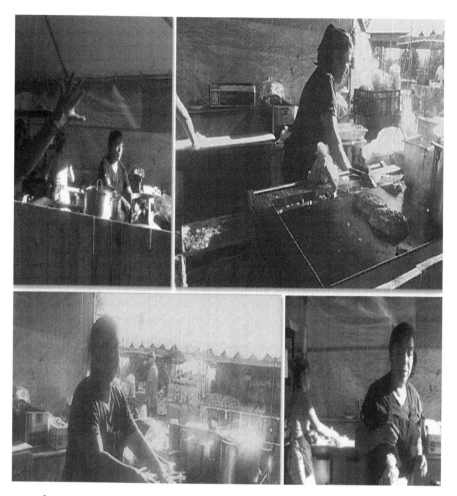

Mamá by Noemi Lara

Our Short History

Nydia Cordero

In my family I have three brothers and three sisters including me. I don't live with my dad, he's dead to me. I love my stepdad, he's always been there for me, and I don't see my mom much because she works most of the time.

People think I'm from Mexico. I wasn't born there. But I lived there for three years. *Pues*, I don't like beans that much. And I'm Mexican, but not like I'm from Mexico Mexican.

I learned English from my father. It was easy I guess. I also went to school, so it wasn't hard. But it has been hard for me to write Spanish.

My dream is to have my career and be someone in life, and have a good life, and to go to college and make my mama proud. She wants me to achieve the dreams she couldn't, and I will.

I think that the most important reason why most Mexicans don't accomplish what they want is because of gangs. Many young people get influenced to do bad things and start bad habits. Most Latinos get involved with some bad people and their friends tell them to do things they don't want to. They get hurt with the decisions they make. Latinos get involved with the wrong types of people and do bad stuff because they feel like what's the point of studying if they don't got papers. And they think they have no opportunity to go to college. It's like a trap, and the easy way out is to give up and be a gangster.

Home Life

Gisselle Lopez

My brother is my best friend, and I share everything with him. My oldest brother is married and has a daughter. I've never been communicative with my parents, and we usually don't get along.

I've always been afraid of leaving this world with nothing to give. I want to leave behind a legacy, my mark. I'm still not sure what I want to do, but I want to be a small part of history. A great pianist is something I would like to achieve, and I'd like to be an archaeologist, and make drawings and artworks.

One of the major issues Latinos in this community worry about is money. Young people are trying hard to get into the right schools, but this is hard. When trying to get a better higher education, people see us as less intelligent than the rest, so problems with money bring us down and make us feel worthless.

I am Hispanic. My parents were born in Mexico, but they came to Illinois, and I was born here. My blood is Mexican, and I can't change that. I have sadly been ashamed of it, for the pure fact that people think less of me and make fun of stereotypes that are addressed to Hispanics. I'm okay with being part of two cultures, but I really dreamed of my appearance being American. If I was, I wouldn't have people asking me if I knew English or not and because being Mexican they act so surprised that I have good grades.

When I began school and interacted with English speakers, they would assume I spoke only Spanish. I never felt bad about that, and it would actually make me feel happy, like I was more Mexican even though my Spanish wasn't that great. I'm a bit disappointed in myself because of my so-so Spanish. All my family speaks it, but I can't spell correctly in Spanish, and when I try to speak it, I tend to add English words. I struggle to express myself correctly due to not being able to find the right words. I don't have this problem in English though.

Growing Up

Maria Ortiz

I have a little sister who's seven and she's super cute. Her smile could light a thousand candles and her laugh that follows would extinguish them all. My mother is incredibly loving and beautiful, but she's really strict. Not to mention that life is never boring when she's around. I have a great daddy who doesn't talk much, but he provides well for our family.

I really want to help other people. I want to get my parents into a better home. I want to travel around everywhere. I want to go to concerts of all genres and meet all of the musicians. I don't really know what my dreams are . . . but I know they are big.

The media does a good job of making the general population of America perceive Latinos as bad people. In movies, Hispanics are always the bad guy or the housecleaner or the dumb kid. I want to see a Hispanic be the good guy in a movie. Why is it that there isn't a Latina princess or a Hispanic superhero? And when Hollywood does make a movie that incorporates Latin culture, it portrays ridiculous stereotypes that aren't true.

I am a girl. A person who wants to be an artist who isn't one yet. I am Mexican, but I think that there are several stereotypes behind my identity. Several of my friends tell me that I don't act Mexican and that really confuses me. To be Mexican isn't a personality, it's a rationality. I am proud of my culture.

I so want to ask her to explain this to me!

You'll Know My Name

Maria Eugenia Cordero Barrios

The seven-year-old girl was frustrated, stressed, and confused. She had to help her mother read and write for applications, forms, and the bills. She would always have to help her with any paperwork. This was a type of situation in which not a lot of children were in because a lot of parents knew how to read and write. But in this little girl's situation, her mother didn't know how to read and write.

This little girl would always stress out so much just to help her mother fill out her paperwork. This little girl would always want to cry and run away. But she didn't because she knew her mother only had one hope—and that was her daughter. This little girl would always try her best to fill out the jobs applications correctly. When her mother saw she didn't understand something, she would always tell her "mi'ja"—which means my daughter—"ask the lady or the young man to see what the paper is asking for." And the little girl would, but that made the little girl feel bad because she didn't know what some big words meant.

One day when this little girl's mother needed her help to fill out a doctor's form, this little girl was really sad because there was so many words that she had not learned. "Why don't I know this word?" she thought. She was the oldest child, and she knew her job was to try her best to do what she needed to help her mother and her brothers and sisters.

She had to help because her mother did not know how to read or write. Her mother never went to school, not even elementary. Her grandparents thought her mother didn't need to go to school because in Mexico students needed to pay for their educations. But her grandmother could not send her because she didn't have money at all. Her grandmother and the little girl's mother had to work a lot to maintain a home, and to make money and food for the family. Just like the way this little girl was doing to help her mother now.

When this little girl helped her mother pay bills, she performed math problems. She practiced what she learned at school. She confirmed with her mother how much money was left and how much to pay for the bills. This little girl was the second mommy in the house because when her mother was working, she had to take charge. For the little girl it was hard, but she knew she had to help out for the good of the family.

This seven-year-old girl would do anything for her family, and she would never feel ashamed. She would work so hard to get good grades and help out her mother with paying bills, homework for her little brothers and sisters, and filling out applications. She wanted to do her best so her mother would feel proud of her oldest child. The dream of her mother was that her little girl could graduate from high school and be the first in her family to graduate college. And with the strength of her mother, this little girl would succeed.

I am Maria Eugenia Cordero Barrios, and this is my story.

Just Me

Kevin Sibaja

My mom is nice when she's not sleepy, and my dad is always mad. My brother is away, my sisters are really stressing. My cousins are the most annoying ones ever. They are fun to be with, but not to be around.

My dream is to be able to have a plain open field where the wind blows slowly. I'll be able to escape from all my problems there. I also want to be a chef that owns his own gourmet restaurant and pizzeria.

Our government doesn't believe in us; they use immigration to take us away. We fight for the U.S. and give our lives to protect it, but yet the nation treats us like second-class citizens. The U.S. doesn't realize that it has no right to take us away from this land and call itself a free country. It's a freedom corrupted by racism. But the nation cannot stand in the way of our dreams and hopes. We will not take abuse, and especially not abuse from those who make us seem like we're an enemy. We're not enemies, we're Americans. We should never be disrespected and told that we can't belong. It's true, some of us weren't born here, *I've been saying this for YEARS* but then again the only ones who were, the Native Americans, had their land stolen. If we should have to leave, then so should all immigrants who have come here. We should all have to feel the pain of leaving the land we love.

I am a Mexican American who would fight for the nation I care about most. America can turn to me, but America can never be able to take my Mexican pride away no matter what.

I'm a Writer, First

Erika Nuñez

My mom is an exceptional person She likes to be part of her culture. My dad is strict, but he loves horses and being outside. He has worked hard all his life, and he continues to work hard as well. My family is from Aguascalientes, and Aguascalientes is where I was born.

I want to buy my mom her house she has always dreamed of, and give my dad a break from all the hard work that he has to do to sustain our family. I want to graduate from the university and be a high school English teacher who inspires students to write.

Many of the students of today have no motivation other than selfish ones. To go through college all by themselves is really bad, without their families. It's also bad to not have anyone to help them or tell them they can do it, not to have someone near who is close to them. This is why family is such a big part of life for students to succeed. Not having anyone is very tough. There are all sorts of things you can't do on your own that are small, but something big like college will require lots of help. Not that there are exceptions to minorities, but there is a big difference in the supposed system in our cultures.

But I am a writer, first. I don't identify myself with race because I am not that. I am what I do, and I am proud to be a writer. I rely on what my talent is and my talent is writing. A writer—that's who I was born to be, and I love me. I can captivate any real or imaginary emotion, here today or anytime really. My words have power.

What I've Learned

Francisco Rodriguez

my family is Hispanic
my brother and sister and me are from New York
but my parents are from Mexico.

there's things I like and dislike about my family
I like how I'm close to my mother and father
what I dislike is how annoying my bro and sis are

one of my big dreams is to play club soccer then pro—hopefully
another one is to become someone successful

I was a former gang member
it's an issue—stands out more as an issue—because Latinos get into this
        stuff from friends as I did
usually from having to be poor or just wanting to be in trouble
        drugs and all the bad habits that are out there for young
        people—
they don't focus on their futures but more on their problems on the
        streets—
it's hard because I walked that path before and was able to overcome it
        with the help of true friends and important people

listen: I am a Hispanic: a person everyone thinks is illegal
        usually people assume I'm from another country and don't
        know anything

Well: once I knew English, I kinda forgot how to speak a little Spanish
        and this land is my land

Beloved Memory

Erika Nuñez

Her eyes harden metallic blue.
Raging screams stomp on wooden floors
"Why don't you look at me when I speak to you?"
Large cold fierce eyes not looking in her direction,
looking at the darkest corner of the room.
Slowly a tiny black head rises.
"Sorry, Daddy,"
she whispers to deaf ears.
A T-Rex shadow flickers to the side.
A heavy hand smacks the side of the door,
and the wind ruffles her black hair.
She quickly stiffens.
Shoulders slumped,
head tucked in again.
If she's perfectly still
he might not sense her.
"You're just like your mother,
a disgusting spitting image."
One on-demand tear rolls down her cheek.
He doesn't buy it this time.
"Don't start crying you brat!"
Tear disappears,
accepting defeat.

Looking at the ghost wall,
lifeless eyes see time's silver hands ticking,
wrinkled skin like dried riverbeds.
Cracked lips that smirk;
the best memory of her beloved daddy.

I Miss You Daddy

Erika Nuñez

I needed you. Did you know that?

Why did you have to hurt me? Why couldn't you just love me right?
Did I do something to upset you, did I do something wrong?

Daddy I thought I was the apple of your eye, you told me I was special.

Said I was your pride and joy, so why did you burn me?

I don't know what to do . . .

I can't count on you anymore, no you're not good.
You're sick daddy, from the heart and from the mind, almost like me.
The difference is I wouldn't ever do what you did.

I know how empty it leaves you, how lost and scared you get.

No daddy . . . I won't be able to forgive you.

I will always be in pain you know.
No one can go back and change the past.

There's something I can only do; I can change how I think.
With that, I can change how I feel every day.
I don't love you but I miss you daddy.

Celeste in a
nutshell

Overflow by Maria Ortiz

The American Dream

Edson González

The American Dream means that a homeless person could become rich, and that a student from a foreign country could graduate college and have a career, home, and family. All this can be accomplished in the land of opportunity. This land provides access to the American Dream only if you work hard and want your dreams more than anyone and anything in the world.

Pursuing your dream can be hard to accomplish, yet there are some people that have the confidence and courage to keep fighting. America gives us strength to keep fighting on. But you cannot just expect to get your Dream from one day to the other. You have to work hard and earn it everyday.

There is no reason why anyone cannot accomplish his or her dreams in the United States. This land provides the necessary tools to achieve all dreams. For some people, all they need is to be good at what they like to have accomplished their American Dream. In the speech President Obama made in the Democratic National Convention in 2012, he said "America your name is no barrier to success . . . because in a generous America you don't have to be rich to achieve your potential." America gave President Obama's parents an opportunity to be successful and to raise a future great leader. I believe in what Obama said about success in this "generous America."

I could say that I already accomplished my American Dream because right now I am happy. And if in the future someone takes my happiness away, I will do my best to reach my Dream again and try not to let go of the promise. I believe in the Dream and no one can take that away.

Life Is Pretty

Maria Ortiz

There are some mornings when I wake up, and, to my disgust, I see a gloomy and grey day outside. Most people, including myself, are quick to whine about the weather. Yet even on gloomy days we should rejoice. Factually, rain is good for the environment and the ecosystem, and in my opinion, it can be spiritually calming. Since plenty of people grumble about something as beautiful and harmless as rain, this proves that our society is incredibly spoiled.

But I'm guilty too. I am one of those people who get angry quickly if something doesn't go their way. One day, I was shopping at Bath and Body Works in search of my favorite smell. I had gone the whole day only thinking about the moment when the musky scent of "P.S. I Love You" would fill my nose with flowers and honey. To my shock, the scent was discontinued. I remember getting incredibly furious because I didn't want to accept that Bath and Body Works got rid of such a lovely aroma. At the time, I believed that the anger I had was completely valid. Because it isn't socially acceptable to get publicly angry, I was mentally thrashing and throwing a fit like a little kid in a store whose mother wouldn't buy her the newest toy.

As soon as I stormed out of the store, the first person I saw was a man who looked completely satisfied with life. I took one look at him and wanted to feel what he was feeling. I wanted to feel happy. There are times when we can read people's demeanors just by looking at their faces. This man I saw appeared as though nothing in his life had ever gone wrong, even though it was apparent that he lived a tragic life. A tragic life, you see, because all of his limbs were gone. He was seated in a wheelchair, and he steered himself using what was left of his arms. Seeing this man was a slap in my face. I suddenly grew irritated with myself for all the moments I had ever complained.

However, it's not just me who is an unappreciative member of society, but it seems like many show no gratitude for their lives and that is easily demonstrated through a huge internet joke called "First-world problems." First-world problems are small daily obstacles that almost everyone living in America faces. An example is, "I went to babysit for an hour and the kids didn't even know what their own Wi-Fi password was." This problem not only demonstrates our obsession with technology and how we have replaced real social interactions with digital ones, but it also demonstrates how ungrateful we have become to have such access. There is also the scarcity that several Americans experience with food, "I don't have enough chips for my dip, but if I open another packet of chips, I won't have enough dip for my chips." What others don't realize is that there are people in the so-called "first world" who experience unimaginable levels of loneliness, hunger, lack of clothing, shelter, and water. Nevertheless, whenever those ungrateful people living in a developed country go a minute without getting what they want, they immediately whine about it. It's ironic because the people who honestly have a reason to complain are the ones who don't, or at least that no one listens to.

The point is that life is wonderful. If you have a beating heart, a pair of lungs filled with air, along with a perfectly functioning body, then you have no reason to complain. If your refrigerator is filled with food and you have a place to rest your head and your backpack is filled with books and friendly people surround you, then I don't understand how you couldn't be happy. Sure, there are several small things that everyone would like to change about their lives to make themselves more content, but when so many across the world are suffering, it's shallow to think about urgent demands for comfort and convenience.

The trouble with our society is that we take small problems and blow them up to huge proportions. Comedian Louis C.K. is right, "We live in an amazing, amazing world and it's wasted on the crappiest generation of spoiled idiots that don't care." Overall, we are given so much to the point where we focus more on what we don't have then than on what we already possess.

An Education Could Fix Everything

Maria Ortiz

I was raised by two parents who have always been incredibly supportive and helpful with all that I do, especially when it comes to my education. They didn't hesitate to get me the fastest computer, the newest books, and the sharpest pencils. My parents don't have the best jobs. They are not doctors or lawyers or entrepreneurs who run a successful business. My mother cleans houses and my dad works at a horse pharmacy. Regardless of how they bring in money, the work they do provides the best life possible for my sister and me. Moreover, they always wanted the best for me. Regardless of the limited amount of money they had, they always found a way to get me what I needed.

In elementary school, I attended a public school. The environment was friendly and welcoming, and I was always at the top of my class. I remember how much I enjoyed the mix of people that attended. I was a friend to people of all cultures and colors. However, it was academically one of the worst schools in the state. There was no structure or organization in the classrooms. The teachers always walked in with positive attitudes and energy to teach kids basic education, but as hard as they tried, they had a difficult time controlling their students. I remember my third grade teacher crying out of frustration because we never followed her rules. It was almost comparable to a zoo. I won't say that I was the best student—because I did misbehave and break the rules. Regardless of my actions, I never failed to get an A on the next test.

After 5th grade, I was given the opportunity to attend a private school. Since I was only eleven, I didn't have much of a choice about which school I would attend. All I remembered was stepping through the door of the private school and already hating it. The entrance was composed of two glass doors with a huge fish tank to the right. I looked at the fish swimming. I remember thinking that going from public school to private school was like a fish traveling from murky and polluted city waters to clear and pristine oceans that sparkled with sunlight.

The hallway ahead seemed boring and lifeless. There was no art on the walls, there was no sound of people's voices to lift up the atmosphere, and the sticky sweet scent that I was so accustomed to in public school was gone. It was lacking everything that I needed to be happy. But I didn't go to school to be happy; I went to get an education. But I soon learned that all the stereotypes of a private school were correct, and I became incredibly miserable.

I still remember my first day of sixth grade. I felt so awkward and uncomfortable wearing a blindingly bright teal polo shirt that accentuated my flabby stomach. It was a rule to have the polo tucked into a pair of khakis that seemed to fit me in the worst way possible. The material was cheap, and I felt like I was wearing paper wrapped around my legs. In order to unify this outfit, students had to wear a belt because, somehow, wearing dreary clothes would improve our educations. As a person who expressed herself through her attire, wearing clothing that stripped me of my confidence and self-esteem caused me to have a lot of bad days. But as they passed by, these itchy clothes became invisible to me as bigger obstacles were headed my way.

The private school was a place where rules weren't challenged. Words such as "suck" had to be replaced with "stink." "Shut up" had to be replaced with "be quite" and "hate" had to be replaced with the phrase, "greatly dislike." Every adult had to be greeted with a smile and the words "please" and "thank you" had to be uttered when asking for anything. The private school was a place where hugs between the opposite sexes weren't allowed and school dances required at least two feet of distance between partners. The private school was composed of people who were mostly from privileged backgrounds who never experienced what it was like to go without. It was not that they were mean or that they hated those who were different from them. It was just that they never knew the empty feeling of what it was like to leave a sleepover at someone's four story house complete with a maid and an elevator only to return to a two tiny bedroom apartment where five people have had to suck in their stomachs to fit in the kitchen at the same time. They never know knew what it was like to be woken up at night by gunshots and police sirens. They never know knew what it was like to have cockroaches as pets because management never cared about the hygiene of their residents and that left kids no choice but to accept bugs as pets.

The worst was when winter or spring break rolled around and everyone shared what his or her future journey would be. Everyone of course would go to an exotic place such as Switzerland, Italy, France, and England. But when I was asked where I was going, I simply stated that my family preferred staying at home because I believed that that answer didn't create a path to asking why. I didn't want to explain that my parents didn't have any money, and I definitely didn't want to explain how I was undocumented. I'm sure it would have shocked them to know that I hadn't even seen the ocean. If these people were told of the poor life that I lived, it wouldn't matter to them because I was not their problem.

The year got rolling, but I didn't roll with it. I wasn't doing well academically. I had no concept of how to study because I wasn't taught how to memorize extensive facts in elementary school. I had never written an essay and was completely confused when we were required to write the format of an academic paper. All the confusing words that had to be learned for anatomy class were extremely intimidating and perplexing. The private school teachers expected high standards from their students, so I had no choice but to study hard and do well. It was crazy how these teachers knew when a student wasn't trying their best because they never failed to ask them after class if they needed extra help. At one point, I got all C's on a mid-term grade report and my teacher scolded me as if I had brought in drugs into the school. Her lecture got even worse when she began talking about my social life. She talked about how I didn't have any friends as if it was my fault that I didn't mix with the people at school. It was obvious that a person who was a shy introvert at an academically average level at this private school wasn't in the right place.

Overall, I was put in an environment entirely different from my own, but it molded me into the person I am today. While attending, I felt like a cheap ugly cactus in a field of delicate roses. However, as time went on and I navigated my way around the school, I grew my own roses eventually deriving the best aspects of the school and incorporating them into my own personality and lifestyle. I may have not had the softest and pinkest petals or the tallest stem, but I was receiving the same education and that was more important than anything money could buy.

At the private school, I learned the value of hard work and determination. I greatly appreciated the love and extra effort that teachers put in for their students. At the private school, I developed a wonderful work ethic that is still with me to this day. They also made me a perfectionist settling for nothing less than my best. Overall, I saw the comfort that an education could bring. An education could replace the cockroaches with a dog. An education would provide a kitchen big enough to fit an entire family, and it could give someone a real house with the sounds of children playing outside instead of gunshots. It could also maybe fix my problem with not having any documents.

An education could fix everything.

My Vida

Ana Castillo

I want to grow up and be a model.

That's my dream.

Everyone has dreams
but some people have
no papers and they have the biggest dreams.

They dream about a job they can't get
or they dream about going to college
but they dream because they can't
because papers make dreams.

And there are language issues.
Some don't know how to speak English and so they have troubles.
They have dreams in one language but not another one.

A Passion For Video Games

Jesus Valencia

What I hope to become after going to a university and gaining valuable life skills and knowledge is a video game designer. I know that this may sound silly and a waste of talent to some people, but this is something that I am very passionate about and something that I truly want to do. I have always loved video games from a very young age. I still remember going over to my cousins' house, sitting on the carpet and playing Nintendo64 all day. We had hours upon hours of fun, and I still have hours upon hours of fun playing video games today. But passion for playing video games is not enough for someone to become successful at creating and selling them. One also has to have a passion for all the arts that go into creating them. I love writing, drawing, music, visual art and I especially love programming. These are all passions that are essential when it comes to game development.

One of my favorite classes in high school has been Sci-fi fantasy, where I learned about the different ranges of genre in writing and filmmaking, and where I learned how to use my imagination to think outside reality and explore endless possibilities. Knowing how to think outside the box is an important skill for anyone who plans on going into any highly competitive industry. Video games are always evolving, changing and so are the people who buy and play them. These consumers want a game that they will want to buy, want to play, and want to tell their friends about. That's how you make money in this business so Sci-fi fantasy really helped me in pursing this dream of mine.

Another favorite class of mine has been Creative Writing, where my teacher and fellow students helped me to learn how to draw inspiration from the world around me in order to fuel my ideas and set to work creating wonderful pieces of writing. In this class I gained the ability to write anything from an incredibly captivating story to passionate, tear-inducing poetry. Being able to bring a player emotionally into the world you've created for them is also an important part of this industry because you want people to love your game and remember it like they would love and remember a dazzling painting or the lyrics to an amazing song. This will ensure that they play it and keep playing it and never ever stop loving it. Players want characters, and I know how to create ones with depth because of studies in writing.

Lastly, I absolutely loved my AP Computer Science class. It was in this class that I was first introduced to the incredible world that is computer programming. I learned all the basics of programming through Java and then some. I'm no expert programmer yet, that's why I plan to go to college, but I love applying all of the creativity and problem solving skills I have to come up with incredible programs that manipulate the screen in front of me so I can turn it into anything I want. It is an incredible feeling. Programming is now a major passion of mine, and I hope to become ever better.

Although a video game designer doesn't seem like the most important job in the world to most people, it does to me. I love video games and everything that goes into their creation. I even program my own video games using a program called Gamemaker. It is not a good enough program to make awesome, groundbreaking games for systems like the PS3 or the Wii, but you can make pretty good computer games and even games for Apple devices like iPods and iPhones. I've made tons of games, and I have loved every second that I have spent working on them and playing them. A career in game design is definitely the job for me!

Shining In The Shadows: A Prologue

Jesus Valencia

The day started out as any other. A warm and sunny atmosphere filled with the mundane smells of flowers, trees, food and water. The air was filled with the everyday sounds of cars and people, animals in the forest and birds in the sky. Everything was fine, everything was normal.

No one noticed the darkness.

It hurtled through empty space at trillions of miles per hour. A shadowy blob, roughly the size of a fist, it fizzled and quivered with a searing hiss. A seed of darkest power, a well of unfathomable depths. It hurtled past the asteroid belt and plunged through our solar system. It passed the outer planets then the gas giants. It tore right through our very sky and continued headlong on its path. There'd be no stopping it, its power was too great.

Slam!

It hit the sun with all its strength, with all its might, and in a flash—it was gone. It seemed to have vanished, just as fast as it had arrived. Into the sun it had disappeared.

Nothing happened.

Silence ensued.

All was as it had been.

Suddenly . . . BOOM!

An explosion so loud it made the planets shudder and their bodies' quake. The tale-tale sign of a nuclear bomb appeared on the surface of the sun. A mushroom cloud that made our Earth seem a pebble. But no ordinary mushroom cloud was this. Darker than dark, blacker than black, it was the shadow of all shadows and emptiness incarnate.

The darkness seemed a tidal wave, a virus of mass domination as it spread across the surface of the sun. Within seconds, the blackness had blotted out all light in its greedy consumption. Now all the light that remained was the faint glimmer of the far distant stars and pretty soon, they too began to fade, fallen prey to the same pitch-black plague.

With darkest shadow all around, panic soon erupted here on Earth. People cried, people wailed and the first few hours were filled with the death of millions. But the panic soon subsided, although the fear did not, and people began to collect their wits and band together. Discussions were made and plans constructed. Life would go on as normal as could be. All would be the same, except for the golden disc in the sky. Now gone, replaced with a swirling cauldron of darkness and shadow.

The Courage Hidden in a Leaf

Jesus Valencia

Summertime,
It hung there waving,
Green lost among green,
Indifferent to the world around it,
Simply enjoying the occasional breeze.

Then fall came,
It hung there frightened,
Brown and orange, sick and dying,
All around, his brothers falling,
But he'll not go,
He'll not be taken.

Winter fell,
A cold, harsh white,
Unforgiving, truly cruel,
A single leaf, on a withered tree,
Frozen over, battle lost,
A simple breeze and down he goes.

Spring arose,
For winter's end,
The harsh white gone in a burst of color,
Plants re-grow and flowers bloom,
And on a tiny twig,
A hero is reborn.

Unwanted

Erika Nuñez

She lays there,
> her head resting against the cool wooden floor,
> a small pool of tears beneath her cheek.

She hears the silent whisper from the other room.

What can she do? This is her place.

Picking what is left of her pride off the ground,
> she continues folding what is left from his clothes.

She heats up the rest of his dinner and takes it to his room.

"Leave it at the door, I don't need to see your face anymore today."

Quietly she sets the plate down, being very careful not to make any
> noise,
> she tiptoed away to the bathroom.

Turning the knob ever so slightly she gets the mirror she hides under
> towels.

Looking at her face she carefully washed away the purple and blue
> stains from her reflection.

Opening Up

Gisselle Lopez

Looking at your faces all happy, fresh. Yet it's the same as staring at the darkness. Realizing I'm just another useless object, so plain and unclear. I wear the mask that shows no pain. Unlike a cold lonely ghost, I have feelings and I'm aching inside, but I might as well be a lost soul because everyone seems to look right through me. I see the smiles on your faces, and I just frown and stumble upon all of my messes.

While I'm falling I try to grab hold but there's no one to hold onto. That just leaves the ones that hate you for being yourself, but they come from a broken home so they are the ones who truly need help. But no one will understand because the words won't come out. They keep on calling my name and their voices sound like venom. Why do they hate me? You only hate something that you don't understand. Life's just another reason for the pain to go on. Staring in the mirror and rejecting what I see, then crying in my bed afraid to go to sleep. Picking up the razor blade, so prepared to let go, when you see the red stains the rest pours from your soul.

They beg me to stop but these monsters in my head just can't say no. When you have people saying they love you it's hard to say good-bye, but maybe they're just lies. Perhaps if they were gone then maybe I'd be free. One day I plan to rise but that day just never comes, this destiny of life is a mystery that will last throughout the ages, a never-ending secret. I'm not an important puzzle piece but perhaps not a piece at all. And if I was, I would be the one lost and fallen in between the cracks.

I'm not a unique snowflake, I'm just like all the rest. Somewhere buried underneath, and every time I have to swallow these lies I feel like I can't breathe. I'm not a piece of work but a demonstration of nature gone wrong. He can't save me, I'm oppressed by the weak lies. They wanted to take my life, and I couldn't let them win because it just wasn't my time.

Spending fifteen years forced and trapped in the dungeon of fiction. Eventually the door opened for me to find the glory of freedom while the sun began to hit the dark depression in my eyes and now that I'm awake I can finally see the light. I don't need religion to tell me my fate, I trust in myself to know the difference of truth and lies, of wrong and right, of love and hate, of peace and war. I can believe in myself to know the right paths. Although we all have our struggles and mistakes, we must pick ourselves up with the help of the ones we most trust to help us go on.

Status

Maria Ortiz

Throughout my childhood my hopes and dreams have always changed. When I was in Kindergarten, I wanted to grow up to be a princess, and when I got to elementary school, I wanted to be a rock star, but when I got to middle school I realized that those dreams were not realistic for everybody. At the time, I did not know what I wanted to be, but I didn't have to worry about it since I had years ahead of me to decide. During my freshman year of high school, I suddenly became scared because I had no clue what I was going to do once I graduated.

I soon realized the scary fact that there was a door closed for me that was open for everybody else who was born in this country. No matter how much I beat on that door, it wouldn't open. I could only open that door with a key and it was my goal to get that key before I turned eighteen. For any immigrant, the road to citizenship has never been easy. Along the way, there are hardships and many obstacles. I have noticed that the few who reach their destination are intelligent.

School right now is my only responsibility. The first thing that I must do in order to receive the same opportunities that everyone else has is to study hard and challenge myself in school. I must show everyone that I deserve the same privileges and opportunities as someone who was born in this country. Even though I wasn't born in this country, I was raised here, I attended school here, most of my friends are from here, I speak the language fluently, and I have embraced this culture while staying true to where I come from. There are many ways for an immigrant to obtain their citizenship, one of the ways is to simply marry someone who was born here, but I will not take the easy way out. I will earn my green card through my education. I'm a valuable contributor to this nation, and I want to give back to this great land.

Another way of obtaining citizenship is to get informed. Last summer, I made the best decision of my life and that decision was going to a college camp for Latino students who are hungry for a higher education. The camp made me realize that anything is possible and that the obstacles that are in the way of achieving my dreams must not stop me from being who I want to be. It is important for a person to get informed because if they don't, then they will never know the opportunities and help that is out there for them. If I never attended that camp, then I never would have known about all the opportunities that exist to help me achieve my dreams.

Becoming a United States citizen is my ultimate goal. I do have other hopes and dreams but none of them can come true unless I receive my green card. There are people born every day who achieve this goal without doing anything, and I must do everything in my power and work hard to get there. I believe that this is only fair. I wasn't born in this country, so I must work to get what everybody else was born with. Although I do think it's extremely unjust that legal status in this country can deprive an individual of so many things, I must work hard to solve injustices.

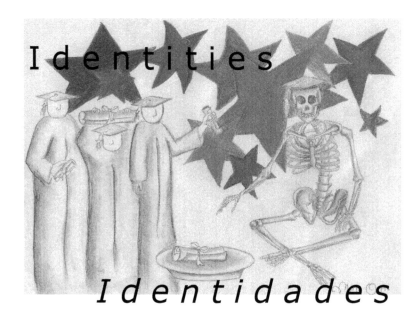

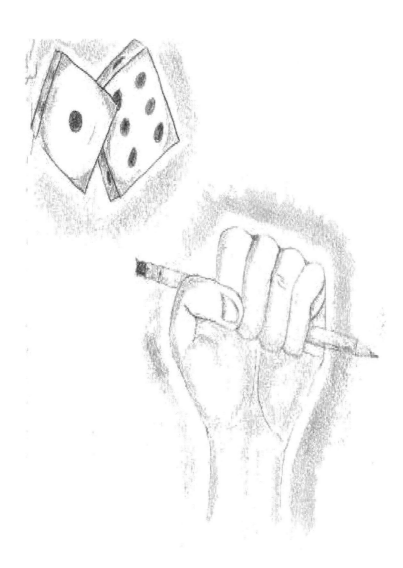

Fight For Your Education by Antonio Sanchez

Hola

Edson González

Los días son largos
y sin ti son más.
Cuento cada hora,
cada minuto,
cada segundo,
para qué te pueda decir
hola.
Aunque solo te veo
y no me atrevo a decirte
hola,
me siento el hombre más feliz,
aunque sólo he vi tu hermoso cabello.
Así cómo soy el hombre más feliz también soy el hombre más triste,
porque solo te vi
y no te dije
hola.
Pero siempre hay una nueva oportunidad mañana para decir
hola
Pero tal ves mañana ya sea muy tarde
 y andes con otra persona que se atrevió a decirte
hola.
Así qué hoy,
iré hacia ti,
hacer que te voltees
 y decirte
hola
Así mañana ya no sea muy tarde
para decir
hola.

Our Raza

Gissell Lopez

Speaking two languages is a misunderstood skill. Learning English was the primary goal for me, and I did this and have done well in school. To get ahead, you have to have it. Try to survive without it, and you'll find yourself with an underpaid job because you can't fight for yourself. Bilinguals sometimes struggle with monolinguals thinking we're not smart, but if we try our best we can prove them wrong. Ashamed sometimes of who we are and only processing the image of what we could've been.

We should be proud of our *raza*, because it's something we can't change. Although it's overwhelming, I need to reach *mis metas*, I want to be someone who matters, a name people say with *respeto*. As time goes on hopefully all low expectations of Latinos will disappear. Instead of being selfish, we should keep on trying for our kids to one day have better memories and a better life.

I Know I'm Going to College

Armando Diaz

My parents are from the state of Mexico, close to the bordering state of Guerrero. My parents are not traditional Mexicans, they're mountain people. And I'm from the U.S.

I'm not quite sure what I want to be. I'd like to be a musician, actually—no. That sounds too classy. I want to be a rockstar. But the chances of that happening aren't so big. And I don't think my parents would approve of that. I know I'm going to college, and I'm starting to like environmental science.

Many Latino students don't have professional mentors in their families. My parents are factory workers for a nearby plant. They rarely have time to ask how I'm doing in school. I'm all on my own for the most part. Fortunately I have a brother who went to Johns Hopkins and has given me some information on college. I can't ask my dad how the ACT/SAT was like for him, or my mom on how to solve a chemistry equation, but I can ask my brother. The guy's taking the MCAT next month. But most Latino students have no one to look up to for school stuff.

Yeah, I'm Mexican-American, but my ethnicity is only a component of who I am, not all I am. I'm open-minded, and I love to learn about different cultures. Even tough I've been to Mexico and speak Spanish, I feel like an ordinary person. I don't know what separates me from others. I've got a rich culture, but other people do too!

Mi Perspectiva

Noemi Lara

Mi familia es una familia muy humilde.
Nos encanta ayudar a otros. Somos muy unidos.
Nos gusta convivir todos juntos.
Siempre hacemos fiestas grandes con bastante
comida. Siempre hay un recalentado al siguiente día.

Tengo muchos sueños.

Aún no se que carrera quiero.

Pero algo que sí se, es que quiero darle todo a mis padres
para que ya no tengan que trabajar. Quiero darle a mis hijos
lo que me dieron mis padres. Que es amor y humildad
y buenos valores.
Los tres obstaculos más grandes que afectan a muchos Latinos
en los Estados Unidos son

1. no tener buenos seguros,
2. la diferencia del lenguaje, y
3. no tener padres con una educación profesional.

Cuando uno no tiene ciudadanía, es difícil hacerle
alguien con provecho porque
no tienes las mismas posibilidades
de tus amigos que son nacidos

aquí. Tal vez no puedas convivir
con ellos porque no tienes licencia
para manejar y entonces haces otras cosas

que no te benefician con personas igual
que tu como ir a tomar y a fumar. Puede uno sufrir
de no saber su identidad porque no saben que pueden
hacer de sus vidas sin un seguro.

I am human just like everyone else, I make mistakes just like everyone else. But what makes me different is my background. I was born in Mexico City. Some people expect me to be rude, loud, and obnoxious just because I'm *Chilanga*, but I like to think of myself as a young woman who is educated and has class. Not all people from Mexico City have to be rude or thieves. And you don't have to think less of me as a human or that I'm a disgusting person just because I didn't come here legally. I believe God loves us all and everyone should be able to love one another and accept each other.

When I started to realize there was a language barrier
I was in Kindergarten. I couldn't understand the songs
everyone felt so joyful singing. When they started taking
me out of class to get help learning English,
I felt so relieved that someone understood my struggle.
I felt so happy when I could ask my classmates to play
with me, and they no longer saw me as an outsider.

With two languages, I have two perspectives inside me that guide me. *Con dos idiomas dentro de mi hay dos perspectivas que me guían.*

Challenges and Pride

Luis Paredes

My family is from Aguascalientes, Mexico. I have two brothers and one sister. My family is really respectful and nice. When we came to the U.S., my mom came with us, but my dad stayed in Mexico. My mom had to raise four kids by herself.

I remember when I started school in the U.S. and had to read English in front of the class. My heart dropped because I just started school four months previously, so I still only knew a few words. The teacher didn't know I didn't know how to speak English. Everybody started laughing. That got me so mad that I started to read out loud and slightly right. From that day on, I said to myself that I was not that bad, so I started to try my hardest in every class. Now look at me in high school and reading like never before.

My big dream in life is to be an architect. I want to have a four-year diploma in the field of architecture. I want to be someone important and start my own family. I want my children to have nice lives with no worries like I had, and that other Latinos face.

One challenge for some Latinos is not having papers. They are afraid of getting deported, and they can't have the same kinds of dreams. Another challenge for Latinos is getting denied by schools and facing discrimination. Another is going to jail. Of all these, I think I most fear being rejected by schools. But discrimination is real. I know this because my family went through this. It's tough finding a new job knowing that you can get fired again and not be able to pay the bills. It's scary. Some immigrants are getting fired just because they don't have papers. But it's not just Latinos, it's people from around the world with no legal documents.

I am a proud Latino. This means that if people use stereotypes against me, I stand my ground and let no one make me feel like I'm useless or not worth living.

Where I Am From

Merari González

I am from two places
one is where avocados grow wild, the other where horses are bred
I am from where bluegrass grows long and free
I am from where animals are treated better than people but yet from
where they are left alone to be free
from where food has a distinct taste
spicy but delicious
where winters are cold and summers humid and refreshing
another where all seasons feel like fall
in both places my family comes first
I am from González and Cipriano
from spicy enchiladas and Wendy's raspberry ice tea
I am from those moments
short and long that seem to last but gone in less time than breaths
I am from here but yet I am from there

Big Rewards

Yasuri Diaz

I was born in Chiapas, Mexico. I was brought here when I was small. When I was younger, I didn't see my dad very often because he was in the military. He didn't come home for months and my mother always felt lonely because my father was never around. My grandparents never visited us, and my mom was always scared that something bad would happen in the night because my neighborhood was violent.

Since my mom realized that my dad was never around, she wanted to come to the U.S. for a better future. And so it happened on January 23, 2005 that we arrived to the U.S. When I first entered an American school they forced me to speak English. I couldn't use the restroom if I asked in Spanish. I felt like I didn't fit in.

Growing up as a Latina is not easy because when a Latina finishes high school most don't think about college. We only want a high school diploma, and we are satisfied with that. It's hard to think about college for my future because my parents didn't go, but at the same time I want a better life. And I will succeed because a high school diploma for me is only the beginning.

As of right now I am a junior in high school. It has been one of the hardest years of my life, but yet I have still managed to make it through. I thank my teachers for this, for believing in me. I believe that life is hard, but if you work hard you'll get big rewards. Never give up!

We Are All Americans

Noemi Lara

1. Although illegal immigration is seen as a national security issue, amnesty for some undocumented immigrants will stop breaking up families, provide for more opportunities for education, and strengthen our economy. We will become a more equal society.

2. Undocumented immigrants walk through an exterior portion of the Maricopa County Sheriff's Office jail, April, 30, 2010, Phoenix, Arizona.
    Racial profiling.
        Unlawful detainment.
            Stalking.

These are some of the inappropriate and illegal behaviors in which Arizona officers allegedly engage. A May 2012 complaint to the U.S. Justice Department filed against the Maricopa County Sheriff's Office argued that MCSO stopped Latino drivers anywhere from four to nine times more than other drivers.

3. Jonathan Cervantes and Angelica Ortiz are two out of the few Hispanic students graduating from their 2013 class in Lexington, Kentucky. Many Latino students in Kentucky get to see their classmates come of age, driving around town with their new licenses, earning some extra cash from their summer jobs at the mall. However, undocumented students won't be able to experience the same coming of age as their classmates. For most of these students none of that matters. What matters to them is earning an education so that they can live up to their potential. Many of the colleges they apply to will require social security numbers. Statistics show only few Hispanics attend college.

4. America is called the melting pot for the fact that it is the land of freedom, the land of great opportunities. Our constitution states that all men are equal. That we have the right to life, liberty, and the pursuit of happiness. Immigrants that are brought to America as kids and raised here know no other home. Yet they feel out of place at times. We all deserve an education. We all deserve to be accepted where are hearts tell us home is. Deporting the millions of illegal immigrants would ground our nation's economy to a halt. These millions of people are working. We have a national interest in identifying these individuals and encouraging them to come forward out of the shadows. They will submit to security background checks, pay back taxes, pay penalties for breaking the law, learn to speak English, and regularize their status. Anyone who thinks this goal can be achieved without an eventual path to permanent legal status is not serious about solving this nation's broken immigration system.

Ser Human

Erika Nuñez

Convincing whispers invade the room
Strings of memory pulled
Forgetting, forgetting,
No.
Not forgotten.

Hidden beneath fictional smiles,
Overlapped by blinding light.

Prayers shoot down,
Useless halos remodeled.
Feather after feather,
Darkening to deathly black

Screams unheard,
Tears unnoticed
Dripping blood uncleansed
How many have passed
With help from fear.

An illusion
Of a hallow life smashed
Shattering crystals
Piercing innocence.

Crossing feeling with thinking,
We are human.

don't cross the line

Ricardo Perez

sí, nosotros crusamos la frontera.
pero that doesn't give you the right to cross the line and judge us.

we are an example of people fighting for happiness.

we can do anything we want as long as we put our mind to it.
     sí se puede
         sí se puede

you call us lazy
say we come here to do nothing but have anchor babies
but without us you wouldn't have America, you wouldn't have our labor

this nation was built on immigrant blood

mi familia y yo hemos hecho de este país.

tu piensas that only because I come from somewhere else I have no
right to succeed in life.

give me a notebook and a pencil, I'll write you my story.

when you read it you'll realize that my life isn't easy and if you live it
you'd be grateful not to have lived what I've lived.

    sí quieren que seamos mejor en este país, denos la oportunidad
de demonstrarles de lo que somos capaces.

give me the opportunity to show you that I can be as great as you, as your parents, and as your president.

I am capable of doing everything you can do, but it's harder for me.

why? because of obstacles history threw at me.

don't throw me obstacles throw me opportunities and you'll see what I can do

solo quiero triunfar,

Y ahora me quieren deportar,

yo no quiero trabajar,

yo voy a luchar, yo voy a triunfar.

ya nomás

Gorditas

Maria Ortiz

With *masa en la mano* and the clapping sound resonating throughout the house, I know that the *gorditas* are on their way. Like a rod striking a silver triangle announcing dinnertime, the music my mom makes with dough and her hands beckons us to the kitchen before it's even ready.

The spicy smell of *picadillo* and *chorizo* dances around the house tempting our tongues and poking our *pansas*.

With utter impatience, we wait in the crowded kitchen for the first *gordita* to hit the plate. Once it's there, it's gone. And finally, the relief hits us all as we satisfy our senses while feeding our souls in the kitchen.

A tradition set by my father, when *gorditas* are for dinner, we feast in the kitchen. We shove chairs and tables inside and eat in there simply because the wait is never short enough.

One after another, they're gone. No more *picadillo* to fill them up with, no more cheese to shape them, no more *chorizo* to fatten them up, no more *salsa* to give them life and no more *masa* to hold the filling hostage. But until there is nothing left, we are satisfied. We rejoice for the blissful dinner with a freezing cold soda and smiles. Little do we notice that for every soft squishy pocket of Mexican ambrosia that we eat, we're becoming *gorditas* ourselves.

Mi Vida

Erika Nuñez

Attention,
Distraction,
How about control?

Lonely unnoticed pain,
Buried beneath empty lies.
Words that were comfort to selfish hearts.

Weightless tears that held no emotion,
Reaching into endless darkness.
Pulling and taking, never capturing.

This is you,
You and me,
I don't want you.

Ragging fire leaps, consuming,
Destroying.
Can we still breathe?

Te amo
I'll miss you.
I see now you cannot be here with me.

Caressing screams tear dark skies.
My life,
My control.

I'm Here: Can You See Me?

Erika Nuñez

They speak of a paper that says my name,
my birthdate,
my country that I first breathed in.
Does this home not count?
Do the 14 years of walking,
playing,
learning,
breathing,
on this side of the invisible line not count?
Did I waste my life?
I have no dreams to them,
I let my dreams fly
only to get shot down
every time.
It's as if
I have no feelings.
I am only a name, and not even a number.
Yet I dream of learning the art of Zoology
of working for this country I call home with a doctor's degree.
One paper will not stop me.
Every door will be wide open for me
I will make it so.
Maybe if I talk loud enough,
you'll be able to hear me.
I have one last question for you.
I'm here, breathing the same air as you:

Can you see me?

Funny

Ricardo Perez

my family is not the best ever
but the food is good . . .

my dream is to have a family
and to be happy even if it's in a little house
as long as I have a happy family

I think hopelessness
is one of the biggest challenges
Latinos face because they believe that they are slow
and they can't reach college
or they can't make it big
but they need to learn that they can't give up
they can still make it to college and make it big
they know more than one language
they can make it far in life

I am Mexican
I see myself as a person who likes to do things different
and I can't change that

when I started school
I would laugh at people

I thought it was funny that they talked different than me
hablame en español I said

The World is Dead

Jesus Valencia

A little boy
Flickering
In the cold bleak depths
Of a dead black void

Sightless white eyes
With nothing to see
There is no light
There is no morning

A dimension without light
A dimension of night
A blacktop of a world
A darkness dripping darkness

Little boy face the truth
The world is dead

American Place

Maria Ortiz

The door opened, and as I walked in to the empty, white apartment, I was immediately drawn to a large window that took up a whole wall. I sat in front of it, and soaked up the warm and welcoming rays of the sun, knowing that it would be my new home, yet being completely oblivious to the fact that I would despise my neighborhood in the years to come.

My neighborhood isn't your typical slice of Americana. When most people think "American neighborhood" they think of the classic cookie-cutter suburban houses where everything looks the same. These wouldn't be the words used to describe where I live. I do live in a unique part of town, but not in a good way.

Where I live, I don't know peace. I don't know what a quiet moment is like without the darkness. It's only quiet at night when everyone has gone to sleep or when it's winter and the bitter air stops people from leaving their apartments. If there's noise at night then you know something is not right. Music is sometimes being played so loudly at two in the morning that the vibrations from my neighbors shake the floor which forces me to play loud rock music in response to their inconsiderateness. During the day, there are always kids playing outside which make it difficult to concentrate on something as simple as homework. Kids, who barely know how to talk, learn their first words out on the streets. They start cursing before forming full sentences.

It has gotten to the point where I am terrified to walk a block to the grocery store. Walking out of my apartment complex, the first thing I see is trash on the streets and beaten-up cars. The smell that accompanies this landscape is enough to make a garbage man gag. If the place where you're living is so bad that you can't even go outside without being sick and afraid, then most people would have the common sense to move out. Due to economic reasons, my family has decided to stay here. But I refuse to call this place home sweet home.

I have been exposed to events that would negatively affect anyone growing up. However, I have seen dreadful things that have been beneficial for me. On the other hand, in the midst of this negative atmosphere, one can always look at the optimistic side of certain situations. I have never had a group of friends who live in the same neighborhood that I do because I don't want to get sucked into a world of drugs and violence. All my friends live in upscale homes with bright green and well-manicured lawns. They live in neighborhoods where the only sound heard is the laughter of children or the occasional dog barking, with no trash on the ground, and the scent of freshly mowed grass. Their neighborhoods are pleasant to look at. They can go out for a walk at night and not be frightened by something awful happening.

I see my friends' homes and then think about how they compare to my neighborhood. I look at all the comfort that my friends have, and I have decided that one day I will live in a neighborhood like theirs. I can only achieve this with a hopeful attitude and an education. One day I will achieve this dream, not just for me, but for my parents as well, because it's important to feel safe and comfortable under the roof that you're living under and your surroundings. I look forward to a day when an alarm clock will wake me up and not police sirens.

I am sure that the only way that I can achieve this is through going to school and being successful at doing what I enjoy most. Things truly do happen for a reason and my neighborhood only serves as motivation for me to try harder and to do the best I can to elevate my family and myself out of this situation.

Afterword

Living Out Loud: Writing the World

Steven Alvarez, editor

In the summer of 2012, several of the Latino Outreach Leaders attended the Latino Leadership and College Experience Camp hosted and coordinated by Bluegrass Community and Technical College's Office of Latino Outreach and Services. Since its inception in 2006, this program has been the only intensive college preparation summer camp and empowerment program designed for Latino students across the state of Kentucky. The camp has provided future Latino leaders with a supportive, culturally and linguistically relevant environment in which to ask questions about college life, to experience classroom lectures and seminars, and develop career goals. The camp also served to improve students' self-esteem and self-knowledge as they were exposed to Latino history and culture.

Sharessa Bentley-Crovo taught a writing course at the 2012 camp, and it was there where she became aware of the powerful stories of local Latino students. She made great strides in opening them to writing narratives and poetry, but because of the brief window of time for the camp, she was only able to briefly tap into the complexities of writing for audiences and textual forms. When I moved to Kentucky in the fall of 2012, I heard about Sharessa's course, and I reached out and offered to assist by conducting writing workshops and editing a writing project showcasing the students' works.

I proposed this book project to The Latino Outreach Leaders in the fall of 2012, and after several classes and drafts these various texts have emerged into the final product here eight months later. These texts reflect the LOL students' viewpoints of growing up Latino in the U.S. Southeast, a relatively new receiving area for Latin American immigrants. Their compositions illustrate the intricacies of writing from their lived experiences as *los nuevos Kentuckianos*.

Students submitted poems, fiction, non-fiction, and artwork to LOL sponsors Tabatha Doyle and Jim Adams, who then compiled them for me to review and edit. Students revised their texts further for publication. I divided the book into sections that speak to different aspects of their themes. The first section "Communities/Comunidades" situates the importance of community as a major factor for student involvement. Related to this, the next section "Families/Familiares" details the central role families have in the lives of the students. This is followed by "Goals/Metas" which offers a glimpse into how these students envision their futures and the importance of education figuring into their dreams. The last section, "Identities/Identidades" connects to the divided sense of self that children of immigrants face as each generation comes to terms with multilingualism and biculturalism.

I'm proud of the LOL students for the hard work and effort they put into this project. All proceeds from the sale of this book will support their club and sponsor scholarships for graduating members on the road to college.

This first edition of *Living Out Loud* by the Latino Outreach Leaders was published in April of 2013.

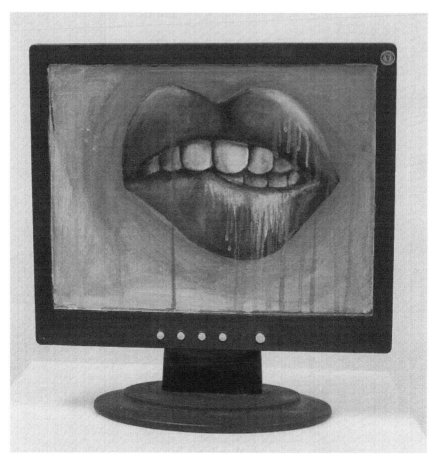

Candy Communication by Maria Ortiz

Made in the USA
Lexington, KY
05 November 2017